Penguin Chicks

by Ruth Owen

Consultant:
Heather Urquhart
Penguin Exhibit and Collection Manager
New England Aquarium, Boston, Massachusetts

BEARPORT
PUBLISHING

New York, New York

Credits

Cover and Title Page, ©Wayne Lynch/All Canada Photos/SuperStock and Bronwyn Photo/Shutterstock; 5, ©Rob Reijnen/Minden Pictures/FLPA; 6–7, ©Jan Vermeer/ Minden Pictures/FLPA; 8–9, ©Jan Vermeer/Minden Pictures/FLPA and ©Bill Coster/ FLPA; 11, ©Gentoo Multimedia Ltd/Shutterstock and ©Fred Olivier/Nature Picture Library; 12, ©Fred Olivier/Nature Picture Library; 13, ©Fred Olivier/Nature Picture Library; 15, ©Exocepts International/ArcticPhoto; 16, ©Rob Reijnen/Minden Pictures/FLPA; 17, ©Bill Coster/FLPA;19, ©Pete Oxford/Nature Picture Library; 20–21, ©Frank Krahmer/Corbis; 22, ©Gentoo Multimedia Ltd/Shutterstock; 23T, ©Gentoo Multimedia Ltd/Shutterstock; 23C, ©Fred Olivier/Nature Picture Library; 23B, ©Gentoo Multimedia Ltd/Shutterstock.

Publisher: Kenn Goin
Senior Editor: Lisa Wiseman
Creative Director: Spencer Brinker
Design: Emma Randall
Editor: Mark J Sachner
Photo Researcher: Ruby Tuesday Books Ltd

Library of Congress Cataloging-in-Publication Data

Owen, Ruth, 1967–
  Penguin chicks / by Ruth Owen.
    p. cm. — (Water babies)
  Includes bibliographical references and index.
  ISBN 978-1-61772-602-6 (library binding) — ISBN 1-61772-602-8 (library binding)
  1. Emperor penguin—Infancy—Juvenile literature. I. Title.
  QL696.S473O94 2013
  598.47'139—dc23
                        2012009605

For more information, write to Bearport Publishing Company, Inc., 45 West 21st Street, Suite 3B, New York, New York 10010. Printed in the United States of America.

10 9 8 7 6 5 4 3 2 1

Contents

A cozy chick

It is morning in one of the coldest places on Earth—**Antarctica**.

A little emperor penguin **chick** has just woken up, but she does not feel cold.

She is snuggled under her father's warm tummy!

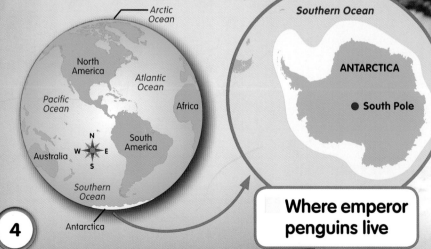

Where emperor penguins live

father penguin's tummy

emperor penguin chick

father's foot

All about emperor penguins

There are many types of penguins.

Emperor penguins are the largest.

They are good swimmers that live in Antarctica's cold ocean waters.

Size of adult emperor penguin

When not in the water, they spend their time on huge sheets of floating ice.

sheet of ice

ocean

Time to mate

Once a year, adult emperor penguins **mate**.

Mating takes place on the ice at special meeting places miles from the ocean.

The penguins walk, and
sometimes slide on their bellies,
to get to these places.

Caring for the egg

Soon after a mother and father penguin mate, the mother penguin lays a large egg.

She carefully rolls the egg onto the father penguin's feet to keep it warm.

Then, the mother penguin goes back into the ocean to hunt for fish.

While she's gone, it's the father penguin's job to take care of the egg.

The chick hatches!

With the mother gone, the father penguin huddles together with other fathers to stay warm.

After about nine weeks, a tiny chick **hatches** from the egg.

The chick sits on top of her father's feet away from the cold ice.

father penguins

father penguin

chick

13

Food for the chick

A few days after the chick hatches, the mother penguin comes back from the ocean.

She has eaten some fish that she will spit up into her chick's mouth.

Then the mother keeps the chick warm while the father searches for food.

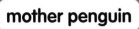

Caring for the chick

The parent penguins take turns bringing the chick food and warming her on their feet.

After four weeks, she is big and strong and can stand on the ice.

seven-week-old chick

three-week-old chick

Now both the chick's parents can spend their time catching fish for their baby.

While they are away, the chick will live with lots of other chicks on the ice.

Time to go fishing

When the chick is about five months old, she grows black and white feathers like her parents.

Then she is ready to walk to the ocean to catch her own fish.

The young penguin has never been in the ocean, but she knows what to do.

She dives into the water and starts to swim!

five-month-old
chick

Growing up

Once the young penguin starts to swim, she lives in the ocean.

She spends her days catching fish with other penguins her own age.

When she is about a year old she will grow her adult yellow feathers.

In about four years she will be old enough to start her own family.

adult emperor penguin

Glossary

Antarctica (ant-ARK-tih-kuh)
the southernmost area of land on Earth;
it surrounds the South Pole and is very
cold and windy

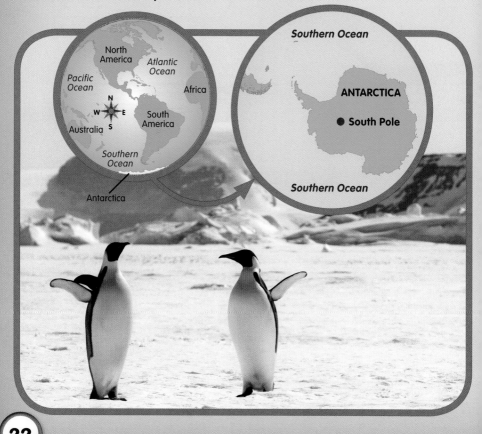

chick (CHIK) a baby bird

hatches (HACH-iz) when a chick breaks out of its egg

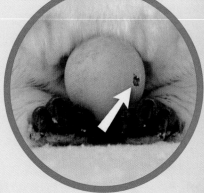

mate (MATE) to come together to have young

Index

Read more

Lee, Quinlan B. *Baby Penguins (Planet Earth)*. New York: Scholastic (2009).

Schreiber, Anne. *Penguins! (National Geographic Kids)*. Washington, D.C.: National Geographic (2009).

Tatham, Betty. *Penguin Chick (Let's-Read-and-Find-Out Science)*. New York: HarperCollins (2002).

Learn more online

To learn more about penguins, visit
www.bearportpublishing.com/WaterBabies

About the author

Ruth Owen has been writing children's books for more than ten years. She particularly enjoys working on books about animals and the natural world. Ruth lives in Cornwall, England, just minutes from the ocean. She loves gardening and caring for her family of llamas.